THE VENTURI ANALYSIS

THE VENTURI ANALYSIS

Learning Better Golf from the Champions

KEN VENTURI
with Al Barkow

ATHENEUM New York 1981

Published simultaneously in Canada by McClelland and Stewart Ltd.
Designed by Helen Barrow
First Edition
Manufactured by Halliday Lithograph, West Hanover, Massachusetts

PHOTOGRAPHIC CREDITS
Principal sequence photography by Leonard Kamsler,
with *Golf Magazine*.
Sequence of Byron Nelson courtesy of *Golf Digest* magazine.

LIBRARY OF CONGRESS CATALOGING IN PUBLICATION DATA
Venturi, Ken.
The Venturi analysis.
1. Golf. I. Barkow, Al. II. Title.
GV965.V45 1981 796.352'3 80-69389
ISBN 0-689-11145-2 AACR2

To Tom Bacon, whose courage and will to live have inspired this book.

Foreword

I could go on at length about why Ken Venturi should be publishing his first book of golf instruction, but I'll be brief and to the point. Ken was not only a very fine golfer—in his prime the best long-iron player I have ever seen—but someone who was always seeking to know as much as possible about how to swing a club and how to make better shots. As a result, Ken today has a truly wonderful knowledge of the game of golf. Better yet, in respect to this book, he is able to put it down simply.

BYRON NELSON

Contents

Introduction

You will not find in this book a comprehensive, involved theory of how to swing a golf club, because I don't believe there is one. The best proof of that is provided by the analyses on the following pages. No two tour pros swing precisely the same way. In some cases their swings are as different as night and day. These analyses are not angled to prove my point either. By simply breaking down each player's swing action, and especially its individual quirks, a total picture evolves with which any competent analyst would agree.

A golfer can get the job done with a flat or upright swing plane, by cocking his hands earlier or later, by flying his right elbow or keeping it close to his side, by using a lot of leg action or not very much. The reason is obvious. Each of us is built differently, physically and psychologically, and therefore each must work out a method for hitting the ball that suits his or her individual, inherent capabilities–a way in which you feel natural, comfortable with yourself.

This does not mean I have no fixed ideas about what is right and wrong when it comes to swinging a golf club, or playing various kinds of golf shots. My ideas are not very complicated, though—and especially not the primary one. No one will ever convince me that the most important element of the golf swing is not the position of the body at address, before the swing starts. From there, as I see it, everything else flows. I describe the correct position in detail, and the body "angles" that stem from it during the swing, at the very beginning of the book. This is no more a "theory" than the concept that in building a house you have to have a good foundation—it's simply common sense. A good player does not get out of swing, he gets out of *position.* High-handicap players are seldom in a good starting position.

If it is as simple as that, then why are tour pros better than average golfers, and some tour pros better than others? The answer to the first part of the question should be no news to anyone. Tour pros hit five hundred golf balls—on the course and the practice range—to every one ball the average golfer hits. Do something often enough, whatever the technique used, and you're going to make it work. The answer to the second part of the question is more subtle. Tom Watson plays better more often than most golfers on the tour because, aside from his natural talent, determination, and constant practice, he creates fewer angles and so fewer problems in his swing. Therefore he has a better margin for error than, for example, Miller Barber, who creates many angles as he swings the club.

I believe this book will be helpful to golfers of all levels of competence because, first of all, the basic address position I recommend can be achieved by just about anyone who attempts to play the game. Secondly, no one will be bullied into *swinging* in a certain way, because there is no one way that would suit everyone's instincts or physical abilities. Each person's golf *swing* is, in its essential pattern and rhythm, his or hers alone—his or her signature. However, within that individualistic framework everyone can make adjustments that will improve the total picture.

You could say, then, that is not so much a book of golf instruction as a book of golf finesse. But don't be frightened—we are not talking about finesse in a highly specialized way. What I'll be calling on most is simply the full use of your imagination, which is what I believe separates the more successful players from the less successful at every level of the game.

In both my analyses of the tour pros and the intervening "Strokes of Venturi" that get into more generalized area of technique, every reader should be able to find a few things that will work well in his or her own game, either immediately or at some point down the road. That is not as flighty as it may seem. Anyone who takes their golf at all seriously is always experimenting, adapting, trying a new idea or going back to an old one. No less a golfing genius than Ben Hogan says that, to this day, he is still learning things about the golf swing. Probably he's relearning or recalling, because in my opinion Ben has thought of just about all there is to think about in his business.

In any case, there are days, weeks, years when as golfers we are different. Sometimes our hands, legs, backs are weaker, stronger, more or less limber. Sometimes we are mentally more "up" for golf than other times. Sometimes a way of describing a bit of golf technique makes more sense than at other times—is clearer, more understandable or acceptable. That's why the learning process is still a mystery, despite all the scientific research of the past few years. How many times have you happened to glance at a golf tip in a book or magazine, or overheard something about grip, stance, or whatever, and all of a sudden it is just what you have been after? You put it in your game and it works.

That's why I like the format of this book, and why I expect it will be one you will refer to many times over the years. The ideas themselves are not original with me, but that's not important. What is important is the manner of their presentation, the language used, the images they may conjure in your mind. There is no strictly controlled, carefully systematized order of instruction on the following pages, beginning with the grip and working through backswing, downswing, and follow-through, because to me the best way to learn about golf is in quick takes—in a sense, by indirection.

Finally, I believe that this book also will

make watching the pros in action more interesting for you—as well, perhaps, as your own playing partners. I expect you will get a little more golfing pleasure out of understanding why Jack Nicklaus puts the club behind the ball the way he does; why and how Bob Murphy releases his right elbow at the top of his backswing; why Fuzzy Zoeller and Hubert Green set their hands so low at address and how that affects their swings. You may, of course, also find a reason to try any of these things yourself—or *not* to try them.

* * *

It is customary in an introduction for an author to give thanks to the people who have helped him, and I'd like to do that now.

Many people have influenced in various ways my learning and understanding of golf, but three in particular must be singled out. From 1952 through 1958, when I was still an amateur, I played at least twice a week with Art Bell, a fine golfer and teaching pro in my native California. From Art I learned the meaning of being competitive, simply because if you could beat him you could beat the world. He was an awfully good player at that time. Ben Hogan was also extremely helpful to me, and a tremendous inspiration. But, in the end, no one person has been more important to my golf career, and to what is in this book, than Byron Nelson.

I met Byron for the first time in 1952, during the U.S. Amateur in Seattle. My good friend Eddie Lowery asked Byron if he would work with me. Byron was playing a series of exhibitions along the West Coast and I teamed up with him for the run. I didn't get any money then, but over the years since that time spent with Byron has been worth . . . well, there's simply no way to put a figure on it.

In terms of basic technique I was a self-taught golfer. Byron polished me, taught me how to analyze shots and swing elements. He painted my whole golf mind. After each exhibition during the drive to the next town, Byron would go over my round, asking me why I played various shots the way I did, and suggesting ways that might be better. I accepted his remarks not only because they made sense and I could *feel* they were right, but because he himself had made it all work so well under the gun, under the maximum pressure that can be placed on an athlete.

A person's mentor does not necessarily have to be a very good at what he teaches, but it surely doesn't hurt, and Byron Nelson was a very good golfer. Byron's record is so well known there's no need for me to say anything more here about him, but I do want to tell one story by way of illustrating his capabilities.

In the early 1950s, Byron came out of semiretirement to play in the Masters at Augusta, Georgia. He was having a pretty good run until he came to the par-3 sixteenth hole, the one with the water in front of the green. Here he hit a 4-iron tee shot that struck the pin on the first bounce. The ball caromed back into the water. He hit his next shot from the drop area, and again hit the pin on the first bounce, the ball once again rebounding into the pond. He made a 7 on the hole, which ruined any chance he might have had for a high finish. In other words, the man just hit the ball too pure, too straight for his own good . . . at least on that one occasion.

Anyway, it was because of things like that that, when Byron talked golf, I listened.

KEN VENTURI
Marco Island, Fla., 1980

The Basic Address Position, and Playing the Angles

Just about everything I say in this book is based on a fundamental address position. I also talk a lot about body and club angles. The two are really married, but I'll define the terms separately and right at the start to put you into my frame of reference.

In addressing the ball you must stand reasonably close to it, generally so that the heel of your left hand is about four or five inches from your body. This gap must be maintained for every kind of shot you play—fades and slices, draws and hooks, high and low shots, etc. You must keep your back as straight as possible and your weight distributed toward the heels of your feet. You bend forward at the waist, not from the shoulders, and keep your knees lightly flexed.

Sounds simple, right? Well, although everybody who tries to play golf can take this kind of posture at the ball, you can see for yourself in a few hours on any golf course how many players do not. Too many golfers stretch too far in placing the club behind the ball, getting their weight on their toes, straightening their knees, hunching their shoulders, dropping their chins. They are pushovers—and I don't mean that only as a pun. Give such players a slight shove from behind and they will fall forward, because they don't have a solid foundation—they are off-balance. In fact, if anyone were to make a perfect golf swing from this address position, he would fall flat on his face. People don't fall because the instinct for survival takes over and they make compensations during the swing. They throw the club outside the line, spin their left hips way to the left—do anything to stay upright. And they hit a lot of poor shots.

They have created too many angles.

Angles. In the proper address position I've described, and which ideally should be approximately the same at impact with the ball, *the shoulders, hips, knees, and feet form a line parallel to the intended target line. The right shoulder will be slightly lower than the left because the right hand is lower on the club than the left, but the right shoulder is still on that parallel. The hands, club shaft, and clubface are at a ninety-degree angle to the target line and the ball. Using a clock image, your hands are on the six and the ball is on the twelve.*

To put it another way, you are square at the ball. If, say, your right shoulder juts forward at address, or your hips are aligned left of the parallel line, you have created angles that will cause a slice or pulled shot . . . unless you do something in the swing to get back to square.

Even if you have a good posture, with the weight back toward the heels, and are square, you can still create problem angles. If you cock your hands going back before the club gets eighteen inches away from the ball, if your left shoulder dips down instead of turning under your chin, if you shoot your right elbow out behind you instead of keeping it pointed toward the ground, you have created unnecessary angles, or at least angles that need other angles to be formed to make your swing work properly at impact.

The more angles and thus the more corrections, the less reliable the swing, and the less likely that you will be square in the thirty-six-inch zone—the corridor eighteen inches directly behind the ball and eighteen inches directly in front of it.

Of course, you are going to form some angles in a full golf swing. Obviously, the shoulders and hips must turn on the backswing and the downswing, and the wrists will cock and uncock. But in the vital thirty-six-inch zone you want to be square, and the fewer the angles you create the easier it will be for you to "be there."

An image: The little ball comes down from the top of the pinball machine. The more barriers it hits, the more angles it goes off at, the slower and more uncertain its passage. If it comes down without hitting anything, or maybe one or two barriers only, it moves more efficiently. Same with the golf swing.

BYRON NELSON

When they say Byron was the "father" of the modern golf swing, it means he was the first great player to take the club straight back from the ball *and straight through it*. Before his time the traditional technique was to swing the club around the body in a more rotary plane, the club coming to the ball from inside to out. This produces a shot with a right-to-left draw and relatively low trajectory. Also, the tendency was to stand away from the ball at address and lean well forward to reach it. If you get to leaning too far forward you can catch the ball with the neck of the club. When he was a young player Byron had a lot of trouble with the shank and was also a tremendous hooker of the ball. The swing he built beat both those things.

First, Byron moved up closer to the ball at address, and since then has often said you can't stand too close to the ball. Of course you can, but very few people do because anyone can recognize playing the ball a couple of inches from your toes is unnatural and uncomfortable. Most golfers get too far from the ball at address. The only player I know who *looks* too close to it is Don January, and it certainly hasn't hurt his game much.

To be comfortable closer to the ball but not crowded, and to maintain good balance, Byron set his weight back toward his heels and kept his knees flexed. He bent at the waist rather than slumping his shoulders forward and thus had a fine, straight-back posture. Everyone should stand this way at the ball, but particularly taller persons (such as Byron), who can take full advantage of their height with a higher swing arc.

Byron's address position pretty much forces a more upright backswing, one that sometimes goes outside or to the right of the target line at the start because you feel you have to get your hands away from your body. Byron did not do this. He carried the club back not with his hands but with his

arms and shoulders *and a lateral slide of his body.*

This slide was what was really different about Byron's technique. It wasn't a big slide, and it wasn't the sway a lot of people thought it was because *his head did not move backward to any significant degree* (his left shoulder hit his chin on the backswing and his right shoulder hit it on the follow-through—and you can't do that if you sway).

The lateral body slide was how Byron got the club going straight back. If you go straight back, you want to go straight through. So, to even things up, Byron made another lateral slide in his downswing. Don't misunderstand. At some point in both his backswing and downswing Byron's body did turn, as it must, but it didn't turn as much or as soon as everyone else's at that time.

Another part of Byron's swing that was

considered unusual was his so-called dip. Everyone thought he lowered his body as he moved to impact with the ball. In fact, he did not. Byron was a slider, not a dipper. Most golfers, even the best of them, straighten the left leg at impact. Byron maintained his leg flex longer through the ball, but with a powerful kick of his right knee he closed the gap between it and the left knee (the gap between the knees at address should be at least half-shut at impact in everyone's swing). In short, it only *looked* as though Byron dipped.

The sliding or lateral movement of Byron's body and his knee flex throughout the swing are what made Byron both a long hitter and probably the straightest hitter the game has ever seen (he also kept the club lower longer through the ball than anyone else).

Byron could curve the ball, move it right or left when he had to, but straight was the main name of his game.

BYRON'S WAGGLE
The waggle is covered at some length elsewhere in these pages, but because Byron had what I believe is the best kind it is shown here. Briefly, the club never moves above or ahead of the ball, only straight back from and straight forward to it, just as Byron intends to move the club away from the ball for a shot itself. Notice also that he never grounds the club—a bit of technique that I discuss later.

A STROKE OF VENTURI

The Mime Factor

Kids get to be good golfers because they are good mimics. They are not afraid to ape the movements and mannerisms of a Nicklaus or a Watson, or anyone else they think worth imitating. As most people get older, however, they become more conservative and are afraid to mime or copy others. There's really no good reason why this should be. Playing good golf takes imagination.

A STROKE OF VENTURI

Intent to Kill Is Deadly

The practice swing is your best swing because you don't think about hitting *anything. Once a golfer has the conscious intent to* hit *a ball—which almost invariably translates into hitting it* hard, *killing it—more often than not he will release his right hand too soon and lose power and control. If he does not have this intent to hit, if he trusts the natural momentum of the swing to produce a well-timed release of the hands and clubhead at impact, he will produce much better shots.*

A proof. When I was chairman of the Guide Dogs for the Blind Association, I gave a lesson to a blind golfer. His coach had told me that the fellow made a good practice swing, but at the ball got so tense he could hardly take the club back. The coach asked me what he could do about this, and I said this would be the easiest golf lesson I ever gave. I said I would get the fellow set up and tell him there was no ball there. I did just that, and he hit a beauty, right down the pipe. Of course, when I told him the ball was there he tensed up again.

Thus the secret is to eliminate that intent to hit the ball—in a sense, to block out even the sight of the ball. This is a matter of self-discipline, and the instruction often given about giving the ball a "hit," or "going at it hard," works against that. You must try to imagine, make yourself believe, that the object is not *the ball: the ball is only something that gets in the way of the club and the swing, something you pass through on the way to an imaginary target ahead of it. That's the only way to get real clubhead speed.*

A good player is conscious of his swing, whereas a poor player is conscious of his hit.

BEN HOGAN

Taken as a whole, Ben Hogan had a unique golf swing that is difficult to copy. The few players I know who have tried to seriously emulate Ben's swing never quite succeeded in doing so. On the other hand, anyone would would do well to copy certain parts of Hogan's swing, in particular his leg drive and how he kept his hands close to his body when moving to impact.

In his earliest years on the tour Ben had a very long swing, the driver dropping down far beyond horizontal on the backswing. He was a long hitter for a man of his size, but also a notoriously bad hooker of the ball. Just about everything he introduced into the swing of his prime years was designed to beat the hook.

Ben had been playing with his left thumb stretched well down on the handle of the club, and he shortened that position to a

degree, bringing the thumb up more on the grip. He also squared his right foot at address, not angling it to the right as most golfers do, which helped prevent him from swaying or moving laterally too much during the takeaway. Then, to make up for this somewhat restrictive position, which could cost some power, he opened his left foot a little more than usual, pointing it more toward the target so he had maximum freedom to make his lateral move and turn of the left hip on the downswing. He also developed a powerful forward driving action with his right leg.

Ben once said to me that if you're going to punch somebody, you're not going to do it with your hands high and away from your body, because the punch will be stronger and more controlled when the hands are in closer. Same with golf. Ben didn't want his hands to get so far from his body that, as he put it, he "couldn't find them." However, he also didn't want to start the club back on the inside, because this promotes a hook. So at address, he set his hands slightly behind the ball, the

effect being that when he started the club back it was moving straight away from the ball. If your hands are behind the ball at address, it's very difficult to snatch the club to the inside on the takeaway. Hogan, however, wanted his hands closer to his body at impact, so at the top of his backswing he changed their position or direction by dropping them down and inward.

Going back, he also kind of fanned the toe of the club out by rotating his arms and hands so that at the top of the palm of the right hand was more or less facing skyward. The left hand will not readily break down this way, won't turn over at impact too easily so as to create a hooking shot. What's more, with his lateral move and leg drive on the downswing, Ben could keep the club going on target much longer, which also helped to prevent hooking.

The result of all this was a fade, although Ben's ball didn't move that much to the right but was more what I call a "hold" shot—one that simply resists hooking. And although Ben practiced fading, he was always capable of drawing the ball at will. He practiced fading because he felt it was harder to do. In other words, like all complete golfers, Ben could make the ball curve both ways—right and left.

Ben had a lot of moves in his swing. In my terms, he created some extra angles that needed to be compensated for. Few golfers can manage this, if only because not many people have ever been so dedicated to golf and willing to practice as much as Ben Hogan. He developed total muscle memory through endless repetition.

By the way, I've always felt Ben Hogan had the most classic finish to a golf swing —the epitome of good balance.

A STROKE OF VENTURI

On Golf's "Work Ethic"

Ben Hogan wrote two things I have never forgotten. First: "There is not enough daylight in any one day to practice all the shots you need to." Second: "For every day you miss playing or practicing, it takes one day longer to be good."

A STROKE OF VENTURI

Golf's Domino Theory

A fellow's stance is too open. His hips and feet are aimed well left of the target, which puts his right shoulder in a very poor position at address—jutting forward toward the ball. This is why he is pulling a lot of shots, or cutting them too much.

You don't tell him to put his shoulder back where it should be. That would get him even more out of whack. What you tell him, is to square up his hips and feet, which are the root of the problem. When he does that, the right shoulder will automatically fall back into the proper alignment.

A person may have several faults. The key to helping him really improve is knowing which to correct first. Catch the basic fault and the rest will usually disappear.

SAM SNEAD

Everyone has always admired the swing of Sam Snead for its beautiful tempo and gracefulness. Not many of us can imitate these qualities, because they are gifts Sam was given at birth. He may be the best natural athlete ever to play golf.

I think that what has been especially remarkable about Sam's long game is his knack for keeping the same swing tempo no matter what kind of shot he has, or the conditions under which he is playing. A lot

of golfers get too fast when playing into or with the wind, or shorten their swing in the rain. The elements never influenced Sam this way, and I would have to say that's because he has always had such absolute trust in his swing. And for good reason.

On the strictly technical side, Sam's swing is not quite as classic as it looks. He sets up with his feet a little closed and the clubface aiming slightly to the right of his target, then gets the ball onto target by delivering the club to it on a path a little outside that on which he took it back. This is a pull, and you probably know from experience that a pulled ball is a stronger or more powerful shot than one hit with the clubhead moving from in to out. And

Sam, of course, was for many years a very, very long hitter, especially into the wind.

Sam can make this move without hitting many shots off line to the left because he gets his right shoulder lower at impact than it was at address, and because he clears his left hip a little more than usual. Other golfers who swing this way might look a little jerky, but Sam does it smoothly and almost effortlessly. He's helped in this respect by arms that are a bit longer than normal and by his exceptionally supple muscles (he's actually double-jointed)—and also because he has great balance. Notice that his weight is more toward his heels than his toes throughout the swing. His extension through the ball is long, and very strong.

ARNOLD PALMER

Arnold would have to be considered the ultimate slugger of the golf ball, but to me that diagnosis is more a matter of his style than his results. Because the truth is that while Arnold in his prime was long off the tee, he was not *extra* long. Maybe it should be put this way: Palmer *looked* like he was slugging much more than he was, in the true sense of that word.

As with just about every good player of the game, Arnold built a swing that would avoid a bad hook. Because of his basically aggressive nature he had two things to work out: first, a relatively fast swing; and second, the tendency common to many physically strong men of getting into a closed position at address, with the body angled slightly to the right of the target. This fortified the sense of strength that suited his nature, and is, of course, a physically stronger position than the open stance.

For Arnold to bail out of these two basic hook-producers he had to keep his hands "quiet," as the saying goes. He couldn't get flippy. This took a lot of willpower plus the gift of very strong hands (Arnold has

always had plenty of each).

The "shape" of Arnold's swing is inside to down-the-line. That is, with a big turn of the shoulders he draws the club back to the inside of the target line, then to get it going on target he changes its direction and comes back to the ball from "over the top"—with his right shoulder moving out a little toward the ball.

With this downswing plane, if Arnold let everything follow its natural course and used his hands in the conventional way, he would pull everything left of target. But because he combined a closed stance with his feet with hips that flared open a little, he could generally hold the club on the target line. In other words, he "blocked" the ball to the target, as we say on tour.

To see this, compare Arnold's right-hand position just after impact with Sam Snead's. Sam has turned the hand over, Arnold has not. And, of course, it is because he holds his hands out of the shot as long as he does that Arnold has the long, high, flailing follow-through everyone has come to know and love.

Unfortunately, the swing Palmer built is not one he could use effectively as he got older, and now that he's in his fifties I've noticed he is opening his stance a bit. His backswing has gotten a little shorter, and he seems to be trying to play more hold, or cut, shots. If I had to name the best part of his technique it would be his grip: his hands look as though they are molded to the club.

A STROKE OF VENTURI

On Gripping— Interlock vs. Overlap

As you probably know, there are two basic ways to grip the golf club. One is the interlocking grip, with the little finger of the right hand entwined with the forefinger of the left hand, and the other is the overlapping or Vardon grip, in which the little finger of the right hand lays in the crevice between the forefinger and middle finger of the left hand.

The overlapping grip is the most commonly used, but the interlocking can't be too bad if players such as Jack Nicklaus, Julius Boros, and Gene Sarazen have been able to use it. In fact, I suggest that when the overlapping grip sometimes doesn't feel right—the hands are too far apart or are somehow "off" in their feel on the club—it's a good idea to go to the interlocking technique for a while, in that it forces a close welding of both hands.

Otherwise, though, I prefer the overlapping grip, and recommend it for the average golfer. One reason is that it puts the left forefinger on the handle of the club and so gives you a little more clubhead feel, this being one of your two most sensitive fingers in terms of "touch."

A STROKE OF VENTURI

Checking Hand Position at Address

The hands are in a sound position at address when their alignment matches and, together, they are not tilted in any direction—when they continue the straight line of your arms. Here's a way to test yourself on this point.

Wear a watch and insert a long, flat stick, such as a tongue depressor, under the band on the watch side. If your hands are too high, there will be gaps between the stick and your skin at each end. If your hands are too low, there will be a gap in the center of the stick, with only its tips touching skin. When your hands are properly set, the stick will lie perfectly flat along your forearm and wrist and the back of your left hand.

A STROKE OF VENTURI

Play to Your Eye

Just as the baseball pitcher throws to where his eyes are looking—the catcher's mitt—so should the golfer's mind's-eye focus on the point where he wants the ball to go just after it leaves the clubhead. The difference, however, is that a golfer's "mitt" on most shots is much farther from him than a pitcher's, and therefore is much harder to keep in mental focus.

Jack Nicklaus has worked out what I believe to be the best way to deal with this. As he moves up to the ball and takes his address position, Jack first looks at his ultimate target, then brings his eyes back along his imaginary target line to a point a yard or two in front of him directly on that line. Now he has implanted a much more acute mental sighting of where he wants the ball to go and can swing accordingly with maximum confidence.

On breaking putts, if your last look before hitting the ball is at the hole, you will probably miss. However, if your last look *before the stroke is at the spot just ahead of you that marks your line, you have a much better chance of making the putt.*

TOM WATSON

For someone who gets his hands as high as Tom Watson does on the backswing, he has the most compact swing in the game. It's a modified Byron Nelson action, and when I watch Tom I see what Byron would have looked like if he had been a few inches shorter. Incidentally, the comparison with Byron should not be surprising, as Tom has worked extensively with my old mentor.

As did Nelson, Watson stands close to the ball at address, a position that encourages an upright swing plane. Tom's is neither an inside-out nor an outside-in plane. He goes down-the-line in both directions, breaking his hands a little sooner than usual on the takeaway and, because of the full turn of his right side, carrying them higher than you'd expect for a player of his height. The overall swing described a U-shape, compared with the flatter or wider arc of Nelson's swing or that of other tall players.

On his downswing Tom doesn't have to drop the club to the inside, partly because he has already set himself close to the ball at address. But neither does he send the club from out to in by coming "over the top"—as many golfers would from his top-

of-the-backswing position—because of his strong downward pull of the left hand combined with a powerful leg drive—good lateral motion and plenty of leg flex. It is a very sound swing fundamentally, the kind that can last for a long time.

There has been a lot of comment on the pace of Tom's swing. He is relatively fast, but so have been many of the game's best players—including Nelson, Hogan, and Palmer, to name only three. Tom himself says that he worries about getting fast, but if he were to try to slow down too much I think he would destroy himself. His nature

is to do things quickly, and he must go along with it when he swings a golf club.

The speed of his swing is necessary, anyway, because of his powerful leg action —you can't be a strong leg player and swing slowly, because it just won't work. Tom closes the gap between his right and left legs very well as he swings to and through the ball. That's important to get both power and control.

If there is one thing I wonder about Watson's style, it is a certain lack of shot-making flexibility. He's very square from address through the finish, and his basic

shot is pretty much a straight ball. However, golf at the tour level is much easier when you can curve the ball predictably left or right, and playing out of trouble or to tight pin placements may give Tom some problems. That may seem crazy to say about the guy who right now is the best player in the world—and it's true that the general conditions of golf courses today really don't require a lot of old-fashioned shot-making—but I'm talking about my perception of the ideal golfer: someone who has an answer to every problem that can arise on a golf course; someone such as Hogan, from whom you simply could not hide a pin.

A STROKE OF VENTURI

On Slowing Down

When golfers swing too fast, it is often because they are in an uncomfortable position at address. This fact becomes apparent to them at some point in the swing, usually during the takeaway, and causes panic and a rush to regroup before impact.

When you're standing in a good position at the ball you love the feeling so much you don't even want to pull the trigger. When eventually you do, your tempo is always a lot better.

A STROKE OF VENTURI

On the "Flying Right Elbow" and the Stout Person's Swing

Jack Nicklaus set a new standard for how golfers of a generally stout or heavy build, or who are at least thick through the chest and shoulders, can swing a golf club, when he gave us what has come to be called the "flying right elbow." By my definition, however, Jack does not actually "fly" his right elbow, but just lets it leave his body. Miller Barber, Bob Murphy, and some other tour pros do "fly" the elbow, and I'll give you my definition of the term in a moment.

In previous golfing eras heavyset players swung the club around their bodies on a fairly flat plane, their hands hardly getting above their shoulders—Lawson Little and Ed "Porky" Oliver being among the best examples. In this way, thickset players could make a full body-turn on the backswing without swaying off the ball—moving too much laterally. In swinging this way they were also following a couple of long-established "rules" of golf technique: first, that the right elbow must stay close to the right side during the takeaway to make sure it was there at impact; and second, that the swing path must be from inside to out at impact. Of course, the shots they hit usually had a low and hooking trajectory. On the golf courses of their time, which generally were hard-packed and dry, this shot got plenty of roll and so gave the flat swinger good distance off the tee. On the other hand, the low draw was a touch shot to hold on the equally firm greens of the time, which may be one reason why there were very few champions who were physically thickset. Incidentally, hard and dry course conditions had a lot to do with Ben Hogan developing his fade, and eventually popularized this type of shot for both fat and thin golfers.

Anyway, as course maintenance improved in the United States and conditions became softer at about the time Jack Nicklaus was getting into golf, it became desirable—vital, even—to fly to ball farther through the air in order to get good distance. Thus, to get this height, fellows with the physical conformation of a Nicklaus wanted to get their hands as high as possible on the backswing, which they couldn't achieve without getting the right elbow out from the body.

Now, you have a "flying right elbow," by my definition, when the space between your arms as they were at address widens during your backswing. Nicklaus does not widen this space and, as a result, his elbow is pointing toward the ground at the top of the backswing.

When the elbow is pointed outward, indicating that the space has been widened, an extra angle is created in the swing and the right elbow must then move close in to the right side on the downswing, or the ball will go all over the lot. This is a "rule" I buy. Thus, if you have a true "flying right elbow," an added motion (or two or three) is required. Obviously, the more motions the more complications, and the game becomes that much harder to play consistently well.

JACK NICKLAUS

It has always been said of Jack Nicklaus that his power comes from the strength of his legs. This is true, but I think another factor about Jack's legs that is just as important as their sheer strength, is that they are not long for a man of his height. This is why Jack can take a relatively narrow stance, which allows him to make a very full turn of his waist *and* get his hands high, both of which have a lot to do with his power and the high trajectory of his shots. If he had longer legs, he would have to widen the distance between his feet to

retain good balance, which would have the effect of restricting both his turn and his arm extension.

Jack makes very intelligent use of his body conformation. He has short, thick fingers and so uses an interlocking grip. His one-piece takeaway, the club going straight back from the ball with no break of his wrists, remains "of a piece" longer than most because he is on such a solid foundation: he doesn't have to worry about swaying off the ball. But, just in case, he does tend to keep his weight more to his left side in the early stages of his backswing than many other players—in fact, you can see just the slightest tilt in that direction. To further extend his backswing, Jack lets his right elbow go away from his right side, the so-called "flying right elbow" I talked about a moment ago.

However, because Jack's elbow doesn't actually fly—the gap between his arms at address remains almost constant

throughout the swing—he does not have to take the club to the inside the way Miller Barber does. Nicklaus simply drops his hands downward as he starts back to the ball and his elbow falls naturally in close to his right side.

That dropping of the hands is in conjunction with Jack's powerful lateral leg-drive, a strong shift of weight to the left and toward the target. The hands dropping and the legs driving create the lag-pump/piston movement that is also a major factor in his power. And, once again because of his big turn at the waist on the backswing, Jack can keep his body low to the ground and retain the flex of his knees through impact—two more contributors to both his power and his high-flying shots.

Finally, Jack is a perfect example of the right shoulder bringing the chin up on the way through the ball. His long follow-through is not forced but just happens, the result of everything that has gone before it.

BOB MURPHY

Many of the tour players, if they had their pick of one man to play the all-time clutch shot when there is big trouble on the left, would choose Bob Murphy. "There's no way he's going to hook the ball," they say, and I pretty much agree. Bob has a good record on tight courses because his basic —maybe his only—shot is a light fade.

Like most left-to-right players, Bob

points his left toe more toward the target than usual—Ben Hogan and Lee Trevino also do that. The difference between Bob's fade and Hogan's or Trevino's, though, is that he hits the ball much higher.

To get a high trajectory you need a fairly upright swing plane with the hands high at the top of the backswing—not the easiest goals for a heavyset man such as Murphy. He achieves those positions by having his right shoulder "over the top" of (or a little forward toward) the ball at address, with his right elbow well away from the body. You've got to take the club back on an upright plane and outside of the target line from this setup, and that's exactly what Bob does.

To hit the high ball you must also make a

full turn of the right side, and Bob has the ability to do this. But the real key is another move he makes, a kind of unusual one. As Bob gets to the top of his backswing he flies his right elbow—juts it outward. This is how he gets that final full, high extension of the arms and club, which he combines with a wrist-cock at the top. The flying right elbow in itself is not unusual, but this way of doing it is uncommon. You could say it's a "delayed flying action."

Bob then pulls the club down with a strong left-hand lead—his right hand does not cross over the left until well past impact—and, as he hits through, his left elbow is slightly bent, the final "block" to keep the ball from going left.

MILLER BARBER

It's fascinating to watch Miller Barber play golf, to analyze his action and to realize that he has won well over a million dollars with it, because even Miller won't deny that he has one of the most peculiar swings in the game.

Actually, the only awkward-looking part of Miller's action is his backswing. At impact he's in very good position—knees flexed, back fairly straight, hands close to the body, and the body well balanced. A very good indication of Miller's fine balance in this photo sequence is the emblem on his cap. From pictures 1 through 8 you see exactly the same amount of it, which is to say that Miller keeps his head very, very steady throughout the entire swing—a key factor in good balance.

The fascination, then, is how Miller gets to his fine impact position. I wouldn't recommend the average golfer trying to

1

2

3

emulate him, because I'm not sure anyone could.

The most obvious feature of Miller's backswing is his flying right elbow—he juts it straight out behind him as he draws the club back. Miller also cups his hands inward, or counterclockwise, on the takeaway, which closes the clubface (and is also why, even with the driver, he never gets the club close to horizontal at the top, despite the full extension of his arms).

Because of his backswing, Miller is pretty much forced to raise his left heel directly off the ground and stick his left knee straight forward toward the ball—this is how he frees up his body to get backswing extension. In all, he creates a lot of angles that take some compensating for the way down.

In regrouping for his downswing, Miller has to plunk his left heel straight down on the ground. This gets his left hip moving directly backward; that is, it doesn't shift laterally so much as it unwinds sharply to the left. At the same time, his left knee makes a circular motion rather than a lateral one. Theoretically, in the "classic" golf swing, you can stand close beside a

4

5

6

door jamb and at impact your left hip and knee will hit the jamb. Miller would have trouble doing this, which is why he is prone to pulling shots to the left.

Miller avoids the pull most of the time by dropping his right elbow in close to his side during the early part of the downswing. This redirects the club to where it can get to the ball on a little flatter plane and from inside the target line. This redirectional move—a kind of flip of the hands—is why Miller is one of the longer hitters: the move gives him a lot of clubhead acceleration through the ball.

Even though Miller does flatten his plane somewhat on the downswing, his angle of attack is a lot closer to vertical than usual. This is why, with irons, he sometimes takes very deep divots. Of course, he must sweep his woods, especially the driver, and to do this he spins his left side out of the way even more.

As I said, Miller has a very complicated swing and he has to practice constantly to stay in the game, which he does. Why didn't he learn to swing the club "the right way," as Byron Nelson once asked him? "Because I just cain't," Miller said.

7

8

9

A STROKE OF VENTURI

On Instant Success

A fellow once asked me how many lessons it would take for him to be a golfer. I said about six. He said, "I'm playing with my boss this afternoon. He thinks I play, but I never have. I'll take all six lessons this morning."

That's a joke, although it really happened. The point is, a lot of people want to correct a slice or whatever in half an hour or less. And, of course, you can usually come up with a gimmick. For example, to stop slicing, put your right hand under more or to the right on the grip and swing more inside-out. You may not slice, but you'll have created even more faults than you started with—and the next day or week you're going to have to come up with another gimmick . . . and then another . . . and another . . .

So if you really want to play decent golf, you must learn proper fundamentals, and take time to memorize them. Without them you have nothing to fall back on in times of trouble.

A STROKE OF VENTURI

Thumbing It

The farther you extend the left thumb down the handle of the club, the longer will be your backswing, and vice versa.

This is a natural physical reaction, so if you're swinging the club too long and can't stop yourself any other way, shorten your left thumb on the grip. Or vice versa if you're swinging too short.

HALE IRWIN

1

It's no surprise to me when Hale Irwin hits a good shot. Aesthetically and technically he stands at the ball as well as any player I've ever seen; he has just about the perfect golf form, with no idiosyncrasies in his setup or his swing moves. I think a lot of this is because Hale happens to have a very regular physique: he's not too thick or thin anywhere, not too short or tall, and the length of his arms and legs is in ideal proportion to the rest of his body. He also happens to be a very fine all-around athlete, having been a good football player in college.

I point out these factors because I think they enable Hale more naturally to adopt the textbook address and swing than is possible for a lot of golfers who are built differently. At the same time, Hale's basic style is worth imitating even if it doesn't come out looking quite the same for you. *If you feel the way he looks to you,* you'll be on a pretty fast track.

A good mark of Hale's classic style is his

foot position at address. Both feet are almost identically angled in relation to the ball, which promotes good balance and body conformation. Hale's posture is excellent, with a slight bend at the waist and the knees lightly flexed. He makes a fine one-piece takeaway with the club, hands, and shoulders all moving together until the wrists begin to cock well past waist-high. Hale creates no strange or awkward body angles during this crucial stage of the swing.

In the downswing, Hale does something that may look unsafe but is actually what

2

3

makes him such a straight hitter. He has what I call a lag-pump motion, by which I mean he begins to move his legs forward almost before there's been any change in direction in the upper body. This is very subtle, but, in the photo sequence here, pictures 4 and 5 are only 1/75th of a second apart and you can see that the left heel came back to the ground while the club was still very close to horizontal. This proves that the lower part of the body is the key to hitting the straight ball.

In the flesh it sometimes appears as if Hal is flipping the club loosely from the

4

5

top, but as these pictures show, his hands are only dropping down a little and in toward the body, which must happen when the legs begin the forward drive as Hale's do. If the hands are not allowed to drop, the club is likely to arrive at the ball from a high angle and cutting across the target line from outside to in. This is known as "coming over the top," and the result is a pulled shot, a pull-hook, or a slice, depending on the clubface alignment at impact.

Hale retains his knee flex beautifully, and presents a further classic example of

6

7

the combined lateral lower-body shift and turning and clearance of the left side going to and through impact. Note that the left leg straightens only after the ball is long gone.

If anything, I would like to see Hale not collapse his hands quite as much as he does on his finish. The follow-through for all golfers is a natural and logical result of all previous moves, and in Hale's case, when the hands collapse on the finish, it means they are close to turning over a little too soon. This can get you to hooking the ball when your timing is off a bit.

8

9

10

JOHN MAHAFFEY

John has made a significant change in his technique over the last couple of years. He used to set up aiming slightly right of the target and, *à la* Sam Snead, pull the ball back on line. Now he has opened his stance, as you can see here, and is hitting more cut shots—in fact, he's become a shot-maker in the Trevino mold, which I believe accounts for him being able to win on such tough courses as Oakmont and Congressional.

At address John reaches for the ball a

1

2

3

little, but not enough to lose his balance because his hands are at the farthest limit of distance from his body without getting his weight out onto his toes. He has a fine one-piece takeaway, in which, like Trevino, he moves the club straight back from the ball before bringing it to the inside.

From the top of his backswing John then drops the club downward before starting it to the ball: note in picture 4 that the club is higher than his head and that in picture

4

5

6

5 it is even with his right shoulder, while in both cases the shaft remains horizontal. This puts the right elbow snugly against the right side and the hands in closer to the body.

Overall, John has developed a better late-hit action, the left hand not breaking down through impact, even though he spins his left side almost as much as Trevino does—you can see John's back-left pants pocket when he's at impact. He prevents the pull or pull-hook that often comes from this kind of action with this left-side turn by leaning his body to the left at the top of his backswing.

By the way, John is another golfer who uses the interlocking grip, whch has a way of reducing flippiness with the hands.

7

8

9

A STROKE OF VENTURI

On Distance from the Ball

When a player who is having trouble asks me for help and I don't know his game and don't have a chance to watch him, the first thing I tell him is to check his distance from the ball at address.

Most golfers, good and not so good, tend to stand too far from the ball. Why? For one thing, we all are a little lazy and naturally prefer to bend or arch the back and slump the shoulders rather than keeping the back straight. Secondly, reaching out for the ball gives a feeling of greater strength than when you are closer to it and standing more erect. That's a misleading feeling, however.

When you reach for the ball you almost invariably end up with your weight on your toes and your knees straightened. Your balance is poor and the tendency is to throw the club from the top of the backswing or make other compensating moves to prevent falling forward.

How do you tell when you're standing too far from the ball? If at address you can't wiggle your toes easily, then your weight is too far forward and you are reaching. You're also reaching if there's no flex in your knees, or the heel of your left hand is more than four or five inches from your body.

A STROKE OF VENTURI

On Procedure

Everybody has a pattern or procedure for doing certain things, such as putting on socks and shoes the same way every day. Such routines make you comfortable, and for that very reason, you should get into position to hit golf shots the same way every time.

For example, when George Archer putts, he first places the club in front of the ball, then behind it, then looks twice at the hole, then strokes. George does this every time, like clockwork, and I believe it is one reason why he is such a consistently good putter.

Billy Casper is similarly repetitive. I've seen him get to where he is just about to start his backswing when something disturbs him—a noise in the gallery or whatever. Casper doesn't then just step back from the ball for a moment before getting back into the address position. Instead, he puts the club back in the bag and goes through his entire routine from step one: the caddie sets the bag just so far from the ball and leans it in a bit, Billy goes behind his ball to sight the line, comes around to the hitting side, pulls the club, sets up, and plays.

That may seem silly, too machinelike, a little thing. But it counts in the score.

GENE LITTLER

1

Gene Littler is rare in that he became one of the game's best players with only a minimal leg drive in his swing action. This can't be easily seen in still photos, because they don't capture the speed and force of the leg motion. However, compare Gene with Tom Kite or Gary Player in the sequence pictures just before impact and you can perceive there is somewhat less intensity in Gene's leg action. Also, in picture 5 his right leg is high and outside, instead of driving low and inward.

Gene's is a physically easy, fairly strain-free way to play golf, which undoubtedly has a lot to do with his making it on the tour for over twenty-five years. Still, I believe he might have won more than one major title (the 1961 U.S. Open), plus additional tournament victories, if he had used his legs more. As it is, he must get most of his power with his upper body parts, and since these are lighter and more flexible than the thicker, more ground-bound lower body, they naturally tend to move more quickly. Thus, Gene is very much dependent on a relatively slow swing-tempo, for he lives in fear of a hook. I can recall at least two occasions when Gene was under severe pressure—when he had a chance to win the Bing Crosby tournament going to the last hole, and in his playoff with Lanny Wadkins for the 1977

2

3

PGA championship—in which he hooked himself out.

A swing tempo such as Gene's is probably the most difficult thing in golf to sustain, because it is so subject to the state of the nervous system. Thus Gene has always worked more than anything else on his tempo, which has, of course, been helped by his quiet, even-tempered personality. Which is to say, Gene plays golf in tune with his nature.

I had better add, though, that he also

4

5

has very sound—indeed, "classic"—swing mechanics. His posture at address is fine except for the knee flex, which is not as much as I would like to see and which I believe is one cause of his relative lack of leg drive. Everything else is geared to his tempo. He has a fairly narrow stance, which requires a slow swing in order to maintain balance, and more of a compact **V**-shaped arc than the longer **U**-shaped arc that brings the most powerful thrust to the ball.

6

7

A STROKE OF VENTURI

Bolt's Put 'n' Take Routine

Tommy Bolt has a way of taking hold of the club when setting up that I recommend to everyone. I think it has a lot to do with his great ability to hit "soft" shots—shots hit with a full swing in which the ball seems to "float" through the air and land gently. This is his put 'n' take routine.

Tommy puts the clubhead behind the ball with only his left hand on the club. Then he puts his right hand on the handle one finger at a time, like someone strumming a guitar. A little adjustment of his feet and he's off.

The point is, when you take your grip with both hands at once, you are inclined to hold too tightly. And you'll tighten the hold even more the longer you stand over the ball.

A STROKE OF VENTURI

On Checking Alignment

I'm not sure how to put this for women golfers, so I'll refer only to men and let the ladies put the idea in their own context.

If you have the correct body alignment at address, your trouser fly is straight. If it's angled over to the right of the ball you're in a closed position, and if it's angled to the left you're in an open position.

TOM KITE

I think that at one point during his formative years as a golfer Tom Kite realized he was not going to be tall enough or hefty enough to be a big hitter of the golf ball, that he wouldn't or couldn't get the power of others, and so he opted to build his game around accuracy. It was a wise decision. Tom could get more distance off the tee by changing a few things—notably, making a longer backswing extension—but I doubt very much if he would be as successful as he has been on the tour. Tom's success comes from playing within himself, physically and psychologically.

The key to Tom's accuracy is the use of his hands. He has a distinct forward press with them (the position he's in in picture 1) and takes the club up quickly with a wrist

1

2

3

break that begins sooner than usual. This limits the lateral shifting of his body and gives his swing overall a tighter, more controlled arc. It may appear he is very wristy, which most people associate with looseness and overswinging, but Tom does not let loose of the club with his left hand at the top of the swing, which is what overswingers do. You can take the club back way past horizontal and not overswing so long as you keep a firm hold on it.

4

5

6

Being the "hands" player he is, Tom could easily have become a bad hooker of the ball. What keeps him from hooking is a very fine leg drive and right knee kick in the downswing. His right knee closes the gap between his legs extremely well as he gets to and through impact. This action with his legs gives him the power he does get, which is ample, and also makes him one of the best wedge players on the tour. He is also one of the hardest workers in the game.

7

8

9

A STROKE OF VENTURI

Good Pitch, No Hit

The greatest pitchers of the golf ball—the best short-iron and wedge players—have not been the longest hitters of the ball and never will be. You just can't be proficient at pitching and also be a long-ball hitter.

Long-ball hitters are long-ball hitters because they get their hands very high, way above their heads on the backswing, and you can't pitch the ball well with high hands.

I think the average golfer would be better off cultivating the short game and the swing for it, unless he's strong and exceptionally well-coordinated and has tons of time for practicing.

A STROKE OF VENTURI

The Correct Hip Action

If you've heard it once you've heard it a thousand times from golf professionals: "Clear the left side" or "Get the left hip out of the way on the downswing."

I say: "Keep the left hip in the way." When you make a conscious effort to "clear the left side," more often than not you will overdo it and end up "spinning out," an action that brings a pull-hook; or, when the right hip moves out toward the ball and you cut across it, a slice.

If you move the left hip laterally at the start of the downswing and then let it turn naturally as you move through impact, the right hip stays inside and in a low position. You'll hit a lot more good shots that way than by thinking "clear the left side" from the top of the backswing.

BRUCE LIETZKE

In trying to avoid hooking the ball, Bruce Lietzke has developed a method that is a curious mix of hooking and fading mechanics. It's as if he doesn't want to give up the distance of a hooked ball, while still achieving the control of a fade. That makes sense, and Bruce is one of the longer hitters on the tour even though almost all of his shots move from left to right. He's won his case, more or less.

Bruce uses an interlocking grip, which makes him firmer-wristed than he might be with the overlapping grip: less flippiness with the hands, less chance of hooking. However, his right hand is in a hooking position, a little too far under the shaft for my taste, whereas his left hand is turned slightly to the right. In all, his grip is now coordinated in both hands.

Most golfers who want to fade the ball take their stance with feet and hips aimed a bit left of target, set the clubface slightly open, and take the club back on the outside of the target line. Here again, Bruce mixes things up. He aims his clubface to the right, aligns his body

square to the target, and draws the club back along a hooking path to the inside. Then he makes a loop at the top of his swing and moves into the ball with his right elbow out from his body and the club moving either directly down the target line or a little from outside to inside. In other words, the overall swing plane describes a figure **8**.

Also, because Bruce is drawing the club well inside of the target line at the start, he closes the face of the club on his backswing. Then he returns it to the ball in a square position . . . hopefully.

Bruce has a lot of contrary moves in his action that are susceptible to error. They depend heavily on good feel and timing, which no one has all the time, and Bruce tends to be an explosive player: hot and winning for a week or two, then well down the money list for a while. When he's going well, he hits the fade he's after (sometimes it borders on a slice). But there's not much flexibility if he's off, or even when he's on. If he needs to get to a pin tucked into the left corner of a green, he has a problem. How does he get to that pin? Very cautiously.

A STROKE OF VENTURI

Turning On

One of the toughest things about golf is that we are hitting a ball that is standing perfectly still, with ourselves also in pretty much a stationary mode. In most other sports the players are reacting to a moving ball or the action of other players, which puts them automatically into responsive motion.

Golfers need some way to initiate movement before taking the club back, and the forward press is probably the most common method. I don't think it's the best way, though, because shoving the hands forward throws them out of the position you want them to be at impact. Forward pressing can also alter the angle of the clubface. You might get the hands and clubface back where you want them, but then again you might not. Why take the chance?

You don't see many touring pros using the forward press. Nicklaus sort of leans his body to his left a hair to get himself started, Player pumps his right knee a few times, and a lot of guys wiggle their feet in place or use the waggle to get moving. None of these motions creates extra, unnecessary angles in club position or body alignment.

A STROKE OF VENTURI

On Slicing

Slicing comes from the body spinning out of position on the downswing, not *from where the hands are going. The hands go where the body leads them.*

JOHNNY MILLER

When Johnny was at the peak of his game, from 1973 through 1976, he was an extremely accurate iron player. Some of that facility came from an early break of his wrists into the cocked position, and even more of it from a tight turn of his right side on the backswing. It was a very compact swing, particularly for a man of Miller's height.

However, when you coil in this way going back, you can't make a good lateral

drive forward—you must spin the left side to get square at impact. This puts a lot of pressure on the left foot, and Johnny's tended to get too far over onto its outer edge, so much so that sometimes it would slip completely out of position. He needed a firmer footing, and if he had come to me when his game went off, one thing I would have recommended was putting extra long spikes on his left shoe.

It's interesting, and maybe more than coincidental, that Johnny won over half his tournaments on desert courses, where the ground is less apt to give way under excessive pressure. When his left foot slipped, his left side moved too far forward and the ball went left. To compensate he then blocked, not turning his left side enough and hitting weak cut or pushed shots. Even in his comeback victory at Doral in 1980 he hit a couple of very short drives to the right on the last few holes.

I'm sure he was afraid, subconsciously, of his feet slipping out and causing him to hook into trouble.

Otherwise, I would suggest that Johnny take a more erect posture at address. It would help if he didn't choke down on the club. He has his left hand about an inch down from the end, which causes him to bend a bit too much at the waist. If he stood straighter the right-side tilt would not be as severe (compare the upward angle of his belt or right side on the backswing to Ben Hogan, who had a more rotary turn), and his head would not drop down on the backswing.

In other words, I would like to see him work into a touch more lateral motion both back from and through the ball. He would still be able to stay down to the ball and get his right shoulder working under through impact, the best feature of his swing.

A STROKE OF VENTURI

If Every Shot Were a Trouble Shot . . .

It often happens that higher-handicap golfers are very good at trouble shots. This is not so much because they have a lot of experience with those shots, but simply because their concentration is intensified. By its nature, a trouble shot better focuses attention: you have *to get around that tree, or over a couple of them, and you think* only *of that.*

However, out in the fairway with an open shot to a big green, the target is not framed as tightly and you are thus apt either to relax too much, to let the mind get too involved with swing mechanics, or to fail to trust your swing.

The "secret," then, is to play all *the shots as if they are trouble shots in which you* have *to make the ball do something very specific.*

A STROKE OF VENTURI

Enjoy, Enjoy

One day a friend of mine hit three balls into the water on one hole and his partner said to him, "Why don't you use an old ball?" My friend said, "My heirs will play the old balls."

What he meant was, enjoy the game. I know some men who are well off financially, play $50 Nassaus, but will try to save fifty bucks by buying junk clubs. Why not use the best there is? It costs only a little more to go first class.

TOM PURTZER

In overall appearance Tom's swing is one of my favorites. Beginning with the address, which is excellent, it's rhythmic and uncomplicated. Tom's body is square to his target line; his left shoulder, left arm and hand, and the club form a straight line at a 90-degree angle to the target; and his posture is nicely erect. He looks to be leaning away from the target a little, but only because he cocks his head to the right. Nicklaus does that, too.

There is a detail in Tom's mechanics,

though, that can cause problems: his left heel barely gets off the ground on the backswing, even with the driver. To a lot of good players this is a safety feature, in that it minimizes the chances for excessive body motion going back. However, it can also easily cause a reverse pivot—the weight moving left on the takeaway, right on the downswing. Also, you can't make much of a lateral slide going into the ball without some heel lift. The tendency then is to pull the shot, especially if, like Tom, you have an upright backswing.

What protects Purtzer from this, and also makes him a long hitter off the tee, is a terrific waist coil in the backswing. This is how he can get such high hands and full arm extension, the club even dropping a

little past horizontal, while swinging basically flat-footed.

From the top of his swing Tom has very good leg drive and his left hip is almost square with the target at impact—great form.

For all that, there is a certain lack of dynamism in Tom's action, which seems often to be the case with beautiful swingers. The best indication of this is his right hand, which seems to be a little too loose on the grip. Check that hand at address and then at impact in the photos and you'll see that when he hits the ball, it has moved a touch under the shaft. With this kind of looseness you're always liable to hit the ball to some places where you don't want it to go.

A STROKE OF VENTURI

A Foundation Test

Hold a club with your regular golf grip, then stretch the club out horizontally in front of you and try to touch someone with the end of it who is standing just beyond normal reach. You can do that by bending at the waist, straightening your knees, and getting your weight out on your toes.

However, if your back stays straight, your knees stay flexed, and you keep your weight back on your heels, you will never make contact with the person you're trying to touch. That's why these are the elements of a solid foundation for hitting a golf ball. Get them right and you simply can't misdirect golf shots by overreaching and lurching forward.

A STROKE OF VENTURI

On Getting Down on Yourself

I once played a round with Ben Hogan in the Colonial Invitational and on the first hole Ben made a 7. When he walked off the green he said to me, "That's why they make eighteen holes." Ben shot 67 that day.

FUZZY ZOELLER

Fuzzy may carry his hands lower at address than any other good player I have ever seen. He also sets the club at address so that the ball is in the neck. Both these positions dictate the type of swing he makes, the main feature being that he raises his body as he gets to impact.

Setting the hands low at address, as Fuzzy does, gives a great feeling of strength, which is why many golfers do it.

1

2

In golf, unfortunately, everything that feels strong is not necessarily good. For example, Fuzzy must stand farther from the ball than I think is best, and slump his upper body. Then, in addition to putting the weight too far forward, he is pretty much forced to take the club back on the outside and up quickly with the hands, instead of low and straightaway.

The swing plane must then be redirected to have the club working toward the ball from inside-to-out, or directly down the target line. To do this beginning from such a crouched address position, and also so

3

4

he can catch the ball flush on the clubface, Fuzzy has to raise his body more and more as he approaches impact. Actually, if you compare his head position in pictures 1, 3, and 6, you'll see that his head drops a bit, then raises a lot.

Everyone moves the head a little in the golf swing, but it should move only laterally, coming up only after the ball is well on its way. Fuzzy's head changes position vertically, which, of course means that his body does too. He doesn't top the ball because he keeps his knees flexed, but, all things considered, this swing

5

6

requires very precise timing and very good nerves, which usually go hand-in-hand.

Fuzzy is a loose, easy-going fellow and nerves are no problem for him right now. Still, his mechanics are such that he can be very good one week and win the Masters, and the next week miss the cut. Also, his overall motion can place a severe strain on the back muscles, and Fuzzy has had some problems there.

HUBERT GREEN

Like Fuzzy Zoeller, Hubert Green holds his hands very low at address, a position that dictates taking the club almost straight up from the ball and slightly to the outside of the target line, and then slinging or looping it to the inside in making the downswing. Where Hubert differs from

Fuzzy, though, is that he sets his weight very much on his left side at address and keeps it there—there is practically no transfer of weight to the right side at all. Also, Hubert's knee flex is minimal compared with Fuzzy's.

In order to generate enough clubhead speed at impact, in the backswing Hubert

has to turn his right hip much more than usual, which necessitates an even bigger loop with the club to get inside for the downswing. Also, he has to really spin his left side out of the way before impact so he can get the club through without pushing a lot of shots to the right.

Hubert's margin for error is not very

high. He has a lot of angles in his swing, and he has to be more "right" in timing and feel to be at his best than someone who makes a less complicated swing. He needs very good nerves, and you can tell when Hubert is not feeling as confident as he might by how long he takes to pull the trigger. At one tournament I counted how many times he pumped up and down, before starting the swing—twenty-eight times. Another time he pumped eighteen times, walked away, stepped back in and pumped another sixteen times before he finally hit the ball.

A STROKE OF VENTURI

One-Piece Takeaway Test

Olin Dutra, the great California pro who won the 1932 PGA championship and 1934 U.S. Open, once showed me a way to check if you're making a one-piece takeaway. It's as good a test as you'll find.

Take your address position facing east, say, then swing the club back until your hands reach waist high, then stop there. Turn to face north and drop the club back to the ground. If you are in the same address position as before, you have made a one-piece takeaway. If not, you haven't.

A STROKE OF VENTURI

On Looking Up

You don't look up with your head when you miss a shot by topping the ball or hitting it "thin"—you change the flex of your knees. You can look up, take your eyes off the ball, maybe even raise your head slightly, and still hit the ball solidly—so long as you don't change the flex of your knees. So, never straighten them as you get to impact.

If there was one thing I thought most about when under pressure, it was to not lose the flex in my knees at any point in my swing.

BILL KRATZERT

For someone with such a wiry build, Bill is a very long hitter of the ball. That's partly because he's a six-footer and happens to be a strong guy, but mostly it's because he has exceptionally good leg drive.

A big key to that leg drive to and through the ball is that Kratzert never straightens his right leg during the backswing. He retains the knee flex, which gives him the flexibility for the move

1

2

forward. He is a perfect example of how to push off of the right leg, and of the effectiveness of that move.

Bill has the fast swing tempo that comes with a powerful leg drive, which also serves to drop the hands and right elbow in close to the side. In fact, there is a tremendous drop of the club, as you can see in picture 4. Bill is a good example of the old-school idea of keeping the right elbow in close to the side swinging to and through the ball. Finally, notice in picture 7 how he still retains his knee flex in both legs when a long way past impact.

Where Bill encounters trouble occasionally is when he gets to feeling too

3

4

strong and then at address sets up aiming slightly right of his intended target. The more you aim to the right, the more you will pull the ball because the instinct coming down is to get the club back onto the target line, which is done by spinning the left side too soon and too far. The other side of that coin is that the more you open the stance and aim left, the more you will shove the ball to the right—Lee Trevino being the best example of this.

Anyway, the more you spin the left hip on the downswing, the more involuntary hand action you get. The ability to delay the hand release is diminished, and you end up pulling or hooking the ball. Thus what Bill Kratzert or anyone who gets too closed at address, has to do, is to square up so that there can be more of a lateral shift to the left and less of a spinning motion when moving into the ball.

5

6

7

A STROKE OF VENTURI

On Fading and Hooking

When you want to fade or draw a shot, do not change your grip or open or close the clubface. Simply maintain the standard distance between your arms and body while changing only your body position at address.

To draw, set up with your body aimed right of the target, and vice versa to fade. The degree to which you angle your body in relation to the ultimate target will determine the amount the ball curves . . . if you let human nature take its course.

Here's a tip on how to get into the proper position for fading, drawing, and hitting straight. For a cut shot—a fade—approach the ball from behind and slightly to the right of it. For a hook, come from behind and slightly to the left of it. In each case you will automatically assume an open or closed position with your body.

And for a straight ball? Come to it from directly behind.

A STROKE OF VENTURI

On Maintaining Your Life-Style

A fellow who always has a drink before dinner finds he is leading the tournament with one round to play, and at dinner Saturday night says he had better not have that drink. I say he had better have that drink—that he should not deviate from his regular pattern of life.

That pattern got him the lead on Saturday, so why shouldn't it get him the victory on Sunday?

LEE TREVINO

To watch Lee Trevino swing a golf club is to take a trip back to the days before golf instruction was as widely disseminated as it is nowadays and fellows such as Lee, who grew up in a caddie yard, made up their own methods. If it felt right and got the job done, what else did you need? "Pretty" is a swing that works.

As I say often in this book, one way or another, it is the position a player takes at address that dictates the kind of swing he will make. There is not a better example of this than Lee. At address he sets up wide open, his left foot pulled so much left of

the target that he is practically facing it with the front of his body. If on his downswing the club followed the line of his feet, Lee would hit everything either dead left of his target, or produce a big "banana-ball" slice. He does neither. His basic shot is the sweetest little controlled fade since Ben Hogan quit the tour.

To achieve this shot from his exaggerated open stance, Lee works the club to the inside on his takeaway, flattening the plane so he can come to the ball from inside-to-out. Then, in moving to impact, his left hip opens even more than it was at address. In other words, his club is going in one direction and his body in another.

To make this work Lee has to, in a sense,

hit the ball sooner, before the clubface has a chance to shut or his left side pulls the club too far left. He gets an early hit by playing the ball back farther in his stance than normal. You know this ball position in relation to his feet is important to Lee's style when you watch him get ready to start the swing. The last thing he does before pulling the trigger is move his left foot an inch or so forward or toward the target (but only the left foot, so his basic hand and head position is not altered). This move also serves as a forward press to get him into motion, but its major purpose is to make absolutely certain the ball is back where it has to be for him to flight it the way he wants.

It's largely because of where he plays the

ball that Lee hits so many solid shots, and also why they have such a relatively low trajectory.

One other thing. In his start-up procedure, Lee also increases the pressure of his left hand on the grip. Cut-shot golfers have to have a very firm left hand, and you know Lee's is because his right hand does not cross over the left until he is well past impact.

A STROKE OF VENTURI

Equipment Check

The iron clubs used by average golfers are usually made too weak. That is, a 6-iron is actually a 6½-iron in loft. This is done by the manufacturers mostly because they know that the average golfer has trouble getting the ball into the air. Also, many clubs are made with too upright a lie. This is done because the club will then tend to catch the ground toward the heel and cause the shot to hook. As we know, most golfers slice and the theory is that an upright lie will reduce that tendency.

If you're a little better than average, you ought to have your clubs properly fitted by an experienced pro who knows your game. Get them suited to your basic swing. I have corrected flaws in many golfers' games just by correcting their equipment.

A STROKE OF VENTURI

On Ball Compression and "Bite"

In 1956 I was playing the Ben Hogan ball and, at the Masters, Ben gave me a couple of dozens balls of about 110 compression. The greens were very firm at Augusta National that year and Ben said, "These balls won't go quite as far, but they will hold the greens better."

He was right. The harder the compression of a golf ball, the faster it will stop on a green. The reason for this, as I understand it, is that the harder ball is more affected by the grooves of the club than the softer ball, which increases backspin. Maybe a better way to explain it is that the harder ball stays on the clubface longer than the softer ball. Either way, it's a fact that when I hit a 100- and a 90-compression ball with a short iron, some paint will come off the 100-compression ball but not off the 90. That would seem to indicate that the clubface makes stronger contact with the higher compression ball.

You should also keep in mind that a golf shot will stop better on a green that is below you than on one that is elevated, no matter what compression ball you're using. The reason is that the ball comes in to a raised green on a flatter trajectory and therefore is more likely to skip and run.

LANNY WADKINS

Whenever you hear the term "hands player," think of Lanny Wadkins as the ultimate example. Just about everything in Lanny's setup gears him to a lot of hand action, and also to a right-to-left shot trajectory.

Lanny has a "strong" grip with his left hand, which is turned well to his right. Also, he places his right thumb so that its tip is completely off the handle of the club, and you can see that the right thumb curls up during his swing and assumes a free-wheeling baseball-grip position. I believe

Lanny loses sensitivity this way, and can't have a really solid, club-controlling grip.

With this grip, and because he holds his hands low at address, it is almost impossible for Lanny to take the club straight back from the ball. Sure enough, the club starts back on the inside with a quick break of the wrists. It's not as flat a backswing plane as might be expected, though, because Lanny breaks his hands almost directly up rather than around his body. He also gets some hand height from a fairly narrow stance, which allows him to make a big turn of his right side.

Actually, this turn is so sharp and Lanny becomes so tightly coiled that he comes close to reverse-pivoting—that is, the body moving forward in the backswing and backward in the downswing. In fact, coming down Lanny has little lateral shift to his left. He moves his weight onto his left foot, but is very soon spinning his left hip away from the target. He also stiffens his left leg considerably in the impact zone. Because he gets so little help from his lower body in producing power, Lanny

must use his hands a lot, and you can see that his right hand crosses over the left very quickly after impact.

Such flippiness can produce a devastating hook. Lanny bails out of this, and gets his shot moving gently from the right to left into the target, by keeping his right elbow very close to his right side as he moves into the ball; by keeping his left elbow slightly bent at impact; by keeping his head down a very long time; and by sliding his right foot toward his left as he goes through the ball—notice the gap between the two is less in his follow-through than at address.

Lanny's swing is a tricky business, and not made for consistency even with all the golf he plays as a touring pro. Perfect timing is everything, and when he has it he plays some truly spectacular golf. However, when his timing is a little off and the putts aren't falling, he doesn't have what I call an "exit game"—he can't readily pull out a 71 or 72 and stay in contention until he gets all of his ducks back in a row.

A STROKE OF VENTURI

The Results of Overloading

When you have too much weight on your left side at address, you tend to pick the club up too abruptly in the takeaway. It is also more difficult to make a lateral shift to the left in the downswing, and you often end up spinning the left side too much.

When you overload to the right, you tend to snatch the club to the inside on the takeaway, which gets you hooking and/or pulling the ball.

A balanced distribution of weight makes for a better start.

A STROKE OF VENTURI

Don't "Ground" the Club

To say you "ground" the club is a poor and misleading phrase because it makes you think in terms of setting the sole of the club as low as possible. You should set the club with its bottom edge exactly level with the bottom of the ball, because that is where you intend to make contact with it. This is especially important when playing from long grass because then, if you do ground the club by pushing it deep into the grass, you must bring it up out of there before starting the backswing. Fail to do that and you'll probably hit the ball fat, or sky it.

If the ball is on hard ground then lay the club on the ground but without pressing it down—never use any more weight than that of the club itself. The next time you get to watch Nicklaus, look closely and you'll see that he just brushes the grass behind the ball lightly as he addresses it.

GARY PLAYER

Size is not as important in golf as it is in many other games, but Gary Player's lack of height and heft makes the great record he has compiled in big-time competitive golf the mark of a man with an enormous desire to succeed. He has a tremendously intense competitive spirit that shows clearly in the way he swings the club.

Gary is one of those who disprove a rule, in this case that good balance is a must in the golf swing. Just about everyone who watches golf must have seen Gary at one time or another practically fall over after hitting a long

1

1a

1b

shot. I once watched him in the Masters hit a 4-wood to the thirteenth green at Augusta National and at the finish of his swing, as he watched the flight from over his right shoulder, his right foot had come fully off the ground and his entire body had swung around far to the left. You don't see Gary off-balance in the photos here, or during his practice swings, because in a noncompetitive situation he is always working on keeping his balance. But the tell-tale signs are always there when the screws tighten.

Gary's imbalance is the result of the tension he develops in his address position. All golfers have to build up some tension or pressure in their bodies to get maximum power and control. Bigger people than Gary can do this during the course of the swing because they have thicker muscles or a longer arc, and so at address can let their arms hang in a

2

3

4

relatively relaxed way. Gary can't wait. At address his arms are tensed, with the elbows very close together. To further wind himself as soon and as tight as possible, just as he begins his takeaway Gary twists his left arm slightly to the right: notice in pictures 1a and 1b how the symbol on his glove has turned to his right an instant after the club starts back.

By now you're probably asking how Gary can swing the club at all if he is wound up so tightly. There are two answers. First, what looks like great tension to an observer is not necessarily excessive to the subject, and Gary is a superb athlete who knows how far he can go before he seizes up and can't move fluidly. Secondly, he is an excellently conditioned man, an exercise fiend, and has developed musculature that allows him to move his body freely and powerfully while under great tension. Finally, he does have a

5

6

7

forward press—a cock of the right knee a couple of times before going into action—that releases some tension.

Because of the tension or pressure he has built up, (and which you can actually see in the expression on his face), when Gary gets to impact he is, in effect, hitting the ball with his entire body. He's the epitome of the person who puts everything he has into the shot—the flat-out hitter. And, of course, this is why he is so often off-balance on his follow-through. Other signs of his potential for losing balance are his left foot—he's well over its left edge at impact—and his head, which has lowered and turned as he hits the ball.

In fact, the head is the primary key to balance for all golfers. Think of the tightrope walker, who can move his arms, hips, shoulders, feet, legs, and stay aloft just so long as he keeps his head still. The same applies to golf.

8

9

A STROKE OF VENTURI

Tension Relief

When Ben Hogan went to Great Britain to make his one and only attempt to win the British Open (which he did), the Scots got to calling him "The Wee Ice Mon" because of his cool, unemotional manner on the course. But, believe me, underneath Ben was always just as anxious, nervous, tense as anyone else who has tried to play this game well.

Ben overcame a lot of his anxiety or tension by sheer force of will, but he also had a little mechanical device that helped him greatly and that can help anyone else. As far as I know, only four or five people have known about it until now, and the discovery took me quite a few years.

A good friend of mine, California teaching pro Art Bell, first noticed in 1952 that Hogan often held the club with the heel of his left hand overriding the butt end of the handle. Art mentioned it to me in 1953, and I saw Ben doing it in 1954, but it wasn't until 1960, by which time Ben and I had become good friends, that I asked him why he sometimes held the club this way. Ben said that with the heel of the hand about a half-inch or so off the handle you can't swing the club too fast—which is the tendency whenever you're in a tense situation or frame of mind—because you simply don't feel you have a secure enough hold on it. The little finger of the left hand is on the handle, and the grip is actually pretty solid, but it doesn't feel like it. You sense you have to swing slower, and therefore you do.

After a few shots, or whenever the tension is relieved and you are back into a good rhythm, you can grip down on the handle in the conventional way, which, of course, gives you a feeling of greater strength.

This is a very simple piece of business, and something very difficult to notice, but it works.

An Image of the Impact Position

The most natural position for a golfer at impact is the same as in tug-o'-war.

Hold a golf club with your normal golf grip and stretch it out to your right at about waist-height. When I grab the head of the club and try to pull it out of your hands, to keep me from getting the club you will pull back by bending your knees, keeping your back straight, and digging in with your heels. That's the same position you want to be in when you are hitting a golf ball, and for the same reason—you have a firm, solid foundation.

JERRY PATE

From the look of Jerry Pate's golf swing you would think he should have won many more tournaments than he has so far. It's such a beautiful action—long, a good tempo, hardly any odd angles. The trouble may be, though, that it is *too* aesthetically appealing.

Jerry's swing has what I call a rainbow arc. His hands get good and high on the backswing, but in the downswing he does not bring them in close to his body—doesn't drop them into higher gear, you might say. There is a certain dynamic tension missing in this action.

I think this is because Jerry lacks leg drive. He has leg *motion,* of course, but not the powerful thrust of a Nicklaus, a Hogan, or a Nelson. This is why Jerry does not play especially well into the wind: he's unable to knock the ball down and hit low shots as readily as players with big leg-

drives, whose hands invariably get lower and closer to the body at impact.

Then, again, this lack of force in his swing is why Jerry is so accurate a player, and such an exceptionally long hitter with the wind. In all, with its one-speed, relatively slow tempo, Jerry's swing reflects his nature, or that part of it he brings to golf. He is in the Gene Littler/Al Geiberger mold—relaxed, unhurried, win-when-it-happens, and make a very good living in the meantime. You can do that very well these days on the tour, as Jerry certainly proves.

A STROKE OF VENTURI

On Waggling

The waggles is one way golfers relieve tension and get their muscles in motion before starting the swing. But there are good waggles and bad waggles.

A good waggle should relate to the swing you're going to make. A lot of golfers, even some of the best—Tom Watson, for instance—waggle up and down, the clubhead going above and past the ball. Tom Weiskopf does this too, and sometimes also closes the clubface—a bad habit. You don't hit the ball that way, and therefore it doesn't help to do it that way as you rehearse and trigger the swing.

You'll never see a pool shooter put his cue over or past the ball when he's crouched down ready to stroke. Instead, he'll move the cuestick back and forth directly behind the ball. That's the best golf waggle, too, back and forth on the same level as the ball, because that's where you want the club to be in the actual swing.

As I've shown, Byron Nelson waggled this way and Sam Snead, Ben Hogan, and Arnold Palmer also had similar, good-looking waggles that reflected what they intended to do with the club in the shot itself.

A STROKE OF VENTURI

When Fast is Good

Fast-moving players tend to play better longer than slow players. A man who plays quickly makes his decision on the shot to be played and club selection well before he gets up to his ball. Thus his thinking is done in advance, and, once over the ball, he simply swings.

The slower player has too much time to think of too many things in the few moments before he pulls the trigger, and for that reason often has trouble: mental uncertainty breeds tense muscles.

I think one good reason Gene Sarazen continues to play so well into his late seventies is that he has never dawdled over the ball. Julius Boros is another good example of a nondawdler. Also, fast golfers are much more enjoyable to play with, don't you think?

TOM WEISKOPF

What makes Tom Weiskopf's swing so beautiful to watch is that it is made by such a tall man. It is unusual to see such grace and even flow of motion in a golfer of Tom's height. The aesthetics aside, Tom's swing is also very sound fundamentally. That he hasn't won more with it is probably because of some temperamental

1

2

3

problems that we don't have to go into here.

When Tom is swinging well he has a fine lateral move back from and through the ball. However, as he starts the swing there is sometimes a little more of a move to the right with his body than is good. He "comes out" of his backswing, as we say on the tour, and will close down the clubface a little early in the takeaway (there's a hint of that in picture 2). But he can usually regroup because he maintains such fine knee flex throughout the swing, and is particularly good at getting his left shoulder behind the ball when he's at the top of the swing.

4

5

6

Because of his height, and his good use of it, Tom has a long swing with the hands high, which is why he can generate such terrific clubhead speed. But his posture is the real key to his power. He carries his back straighter than any other tall man in the game—and also straighter than most shorter players. This is the secret to his excellent balance, and a good measure of it is the fact that his head position at impact is almost exactly the same as it was at address. Compare his balance with that of Gary Player, Johnny Miller, Lanny Wadkins, and Raymond Floyd—fellows who are not as tall as Tom and yet have some trouble with retaining their balance.

7

8

9

A STROKE OF VENTURI

On Physical Conditioning

Jack Nicklaus is one of the few golfers I know who changed his physical proportions fairly drastically—in his case by losing a lot of weight—and still retained his swing and the quality of his game. But Jack is probably a special case in that respect, as he is in so many other ways. My feeling generally is that if you're at a certain weight and shooting good scores, stay there. If you're determined to lose weight, at least wait until you're not playing well. I know a number of fellows who were heavyset and had good runs on the tour, but were never heard from again after they got the "be-thin" syndrome.

When I was at the peak of my game, my legs got a rubdown but that was all. I never had the back of my neck, my shoulders, or my arms touched. I didn't want to fool with my golf muscle-tone.

If you're going to do some exercise to lose weight, or to feel better, or whatever, make it work for your golf. For example, swimming is awful for golf because nowhere in the golf swing do your arms come over the top. Tennis is the same—especially the serve and overhead—plus the fact that you use only one hand which gets either overstrong or overtired for golf. The muscles used for parallel bars, rings, and other gymnasium equipment are not used for golf, and excerises on them will also be detrimental to your golf game.

If you want to be a jack-of-all-trades, you'll almost certainly be a master of none.

A STROKE OF VENTURI

The One-Piece Tempo

If your takeaway is a good, one-piece action—the hands, clubhead, and shoulders moving together until the hands get waist high before they begin to break—your swing tempo **has** ***to be slower. By moving one part at a time—say, the hands—you have to be quicker, simply because it's easier to move one part of the body than three or four parts at once.***

1

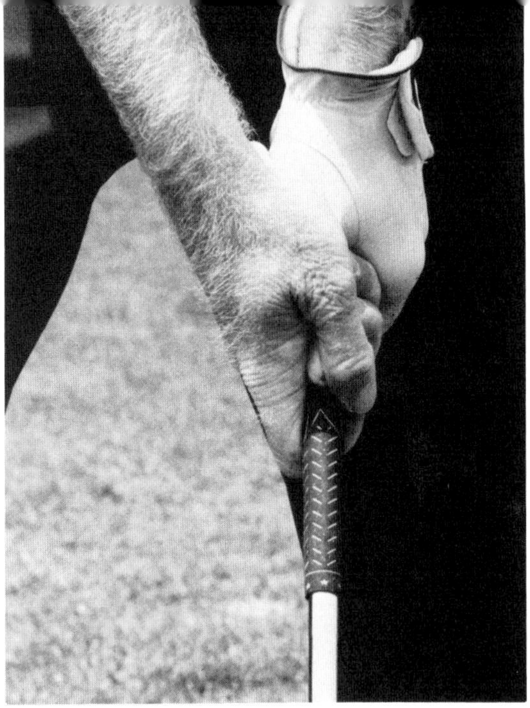

ANDY BEAN

Andy has an unusual grip on the club, extending his left thumb so far down the shaft that it can be seen between the thumb and forefinger of the right hand. The close-up picture of his grip shows this well.

This is an extreme example of welding the hands close together so they work in unison, and I think it's something Andy picked up to avoid hooking the ball. In order to get the thumb as far down the

2

3

shaft as he does, you must tilt your left hand upward. Most people who tilt the hand that way will push the ball to the right. Andy doesn't push the ball, or hook excessively, because he is strong enough to make this grip work for him.

In fact, no one in the game deals more from sheer strength than Andy, who is a very big and a very strong man. A long hitter, he gets his distance chiefly from his strength, because for a man of his height (6'4") he has neither a long backswing extension or a particularly power-producing swing plane. His action is pretty much straight up-and-down, with very little lateral motion and not even much of a turn of the right side. His left heel rarely leaves the ground on the backswing.

Andy's left shoulder works under his head and sort of dips down toward the ball, rather than getting behind it. His hands are high, but never too far from his body. He has a terrific kick with his right knee as he gets to impact, but is not moving his hips too much to the left. As I say, you have to be a very strong man to get the distance Andy does with the swing he makes.

The one criticism I would make of Andy's style is that he goes from a very good position in picture 5, with a great knee flex and lateral drive, to a poor

4

5

position in picture 7, in which his body has tilted backward and his head has gone down as well as backward. To see how much his head moves, look at where it is in relation to the white spot to his right in pictures 5 and 7.

For a man who keeps his feet on the ground so well early in the downswing, he gets up on the toes of his right foot a little too soon. Here he has gone from a strong position to a weaker one, in that he is flipping the club with his hands—you can see in the picture 7 how his right hand is crossing over already.

The head movement and body tilt, and the hands flipping, are why Andy's shots generally have a kind of rainbow trajectory, the ball reaching its maximum height in the middle of its flight. I prefer a "riser," a shot that bores a little lower early on and reaches its apex nearer the end of its flight. The riser is less apt to be affected by the wind, and it lands much more softly.

6

7

8

A STROKE OF VENTURI

Golf Is a Variety Show

Try to play golf with only one kind of shot—a draw, a fade, a high ball or low ball—and you'll have nothing to turn to when you don't have your stuff on a particular day.

When you go sour, as everyone does at times, try something that works for the moment—pull something out of your armory of shots to get you through the day—then go back and work on the things you really want to do.

Working on a variety of shots when practicing is valuable, and makes the workout more fun, too.

A STROKE OF VENTURI

The Right Order of Thoughts

We all know where we want the ball to go and where we don't want it to go. Good players put this in the proper sequence. They go from the negative to the positive. Let's say you have an approach to a green with water on the right side. The wrong-thinking player will say, "I would like to get on the green and there's less trouble on the left, but I don't want to go in the water on the right." Often he goes in the water on the right because his very last thought before taking the club back was a negative one.

The right-thinking golfer says, "I don't want to go right. I need to do this, this, and this to get on the green." Usually that's where he puts it.

A STROKE OF VENTURI

Playing "Lay-Up" All the Way

I've done this with a lot of golfers, pros and amateurs. I say to them, "Hit six balls as hard as you can. Then hit six more and say to yourself that you don't want any of these to go past any of the first six."

Every one of the last six balls will equal or pass the shortest of the first six balls. Why? Because the golfer has swung easier, with better tempo, as when laying up short of trouble.

So what do you do when really *laying up? Use less club.*

A STROKE VENTURI

On Clubbing Yourself

Except for the driver, the golf clubs we use are designed to hit the ball certain distances—125 yards with a 9-iron, 155 yards with a 6-iron, and so on. But such distances are only a general frame of reference. Everyone hits the ball a little differently, and what every golfer should do is find his own specific distances.

Hit six or seven shots with each of your clubs, under ideal, windless conditions, then step them off and find your average with each club. If you hit a 5-iron only 135 yards, accept the fact and live with it. Obviously you'll have to make allowances for wind and other factors, but even then you'll be working from the basis of a specific known value, which is a lot better than always guessing.

My own club distances are spaced eleven yards, beginning with a 125-yard 9-iron.

MARK HAYES

Although it can't be caught by still photography, Mark Hayes has a slight pause at the top of his backswing that is reminiscent of Gary Middlecoff, although the pause is not as pronounced.

A pause at the top tends to create some tension in the hands and arms, and because of this the club is apt to be brought to the ball from outside the intended line of flight—"over the top"—which can produce a pull or pull-hook.

You can pause this way only by making a relatively slow backswing, and, as with Gene Littler and Al Geiberger, tempo then becomes the prime concern in order to get power and control. I've always felt that, as you get close to the top of the backswing,

1

2

3

you should start the hips moving forward, as Ben Hogan and many other top players have done. With this lag-pump, pistonlike action you may swing a little faster, overall, but the hands almost automatically drop closer to the body for more shot control and a more natural power flow.

Mark Hayes is not a short hitter—in fact, he is probably the longest short-iron hitter on the circuit. I once saw him hit a 180-yard 8-iron, and not downwind. He can do that because he has terrific hand-speed in the impact zone—possibly the fastest hand release on tour.

Mark needs to whip his hands in the way to make up for his slow backswing tempo and pause at the top, and because he doesn't have a real good coil of his upper body, as you can see by comparing him in picture 3 with, for example, Jack Nicklaus at the same point in the swing.

In moving into the ball, Mark has to have

4

5

6

well-coordinated hand and knee action—and he does. He's up on his right toes midway through the downswing, because his leg drive is so strong. And with his left side so far ahead, he has to move his hands rapidly into impact.

This is fine when it works, but it requires acute timing, which may account for some peaks and valleys in Mark's overall tour performance. Also, Mark's shots get very high, especially with the shorter irons, which isn't ideal under windy conditions. It's hard for him to play three-quarter knockdown shots with his kind of super-lively hand action, and he's best when going at the ball full bore.

Finally, as a result of the quickness of his hands through the ball, he finds it hard to get a long arm extension after impact, and there is a lot of arching of the back at the finish, which in time can cause physical problems.

7

8

9

A STROKE OF VENTURI

On Pitching with Your Legs

Leg action is the key to pitching the ball well. The faster you move the right knee toward the left leg in the downswing, the more spin you will put on the ball. You'll get softer shots, too. With no leg action, you work your hands and hit a lot of shots with less spin or bite on them.

A STROKE OF VENTURI

"At Home" Holes

Some golf holes "fit your eye" better than others. The shape of the hole, the angle of the fairway, the ways the trees are situated, the height of the tree in relation to the fairway or green, or whatever else it may be, makes you feel comfortable—"at home." And you almost invariably play such holes well.

Then there are those holes that don't fit your eye, that you never like, and that, as a result, play tougher than they actually are. In such cases I recommend trying to do something different with the ball to add a special challenge to the hole that will make you bear down harder.

A STROKE OF VENTURI

On "Looking" Good

When you're playing well, you're looking at where you want the ball to go. When you're playing poorly, you're looking at where you don't want to go.

The trick is to look only where you want the ball to go, even when you're not playing well.

A STROKE OF VENTURI

The Plank Theory

When you walk a two-by-four you walk slowly because you are trying to keep your balance. Walk a ten-by-four and you move more quickly and surely because you have more room and can keep your feet wider apart.

The same applies to golf. If your feet are close together you must work more to maintain balance; thus, you must swing slower and less powerfully.

RAYMOND FLOYD

Raymond is thickly built through the shoulders and chest, which makes it a little difficult to get the full backswing extension and high hands he wants *without flying his right elbow*.

To get that extension, Raymond keeps the club very low at the start of his takeaway—the clubhead is lower than his pants cuffs until it gets past his right foot. He also gets full arm extension and high hands while avoiding a sway by keeping a

1

2

3

good knee flex and, after the low initial takeaway, lifting the club almost straight up with the cocking of his hands.

However, at the top Raymond gets up on the toes of his left foot, rather than having his weight predominantly along its inside edge. This raises his left heel a little higher than normal and, for stability in his downswing, he has to set the left heel back down rather abruptly. It's a move that includes a snap of his head back to where it was at address, which gives his swing at this point a jerky look.

Also, to get his left knee into the position it's in in picture 5, it must circle around, which works against a good lateral move to the left. Thus the left leg straightens at impact, and there is potential in this for spinning out, for making a too-sharp turn of the left side away from the

4

5

ball. Raymond counters this with a strong kick targetward of his right knee, at the same time making a good long extension of his hands and the club through the ball and toward the target. He also stays behind the ball well, as you can see by the position of his head at impact. By staying well back with the club low and long through the ball, and by not letting his left hand collapse—in picture 6 you can see how the back of it is facing the target—Raymond can fly the ball well up into the air. That's why he's such a fine fairway wood player.

Raymond is a fine example of a player who looks "under" the ball when following its flight. This is the mark of someone who has stayed down and swung his right shoulder under his chin through impact.

6

7

A STROKE OF VENTURI

Manager Hogan

The idea of always going for broke on the golf course is put in its place by a story Dick Siderowf, the fine amateur golfer, once told me about Ben Hogan. It also typified Ben's course management, and his supreme self-confidence.

Siderowf was playing just ahead of Hogan at the Masters, and on the par-5 thirteenth both drove to almost the identical spot in the fairway. Siderowf had hit his second shot onto the green with a 3-wood, carrying the pond fronting the putting surface. Dick noticed that Hogan layed up short of the water. After the round Dick asked Ben why he layed up on the thirteenth when he could have gotten home with a wood. Hogan said, "I didn't need a three." By the way, Ben made a 4.

A STROKE OF VENTURI

High Ball, Low Ball

To hit a golf shot higher or lower than normal, the only thing you need do is change your foot position at address—shifting the ball more toward the left heel for the high one and more toward the right heel for the low one. That is not big news in itself, but there is a trick to doing it right. Too many golfers will get into either of these positions by adjusting *both* feet. That's chancy, because you may not get it right.

First, take your normal position at the ball. Then, for the high shot, move *only* the right foot back. For the low shot, move *only* the left foot forward. In this way you are keeping the ball and your head in the same basic position to make solid contact.

CHI-CHI RODRIGUEZ

There are a few specially good bunker players on the tour, but if I had to pick one man to play *the* sand shot that meant it all, Chi-Chi would get my nod. His technique is excellent for short bunker shots. It may not be quite so good for longer explosions, but that doesn't matter because no one gets very many of those and no one can play them consistently well, anyway.

Chi-Chi sets the blade of the wedge open so that the heel is the first part to enter the sand. He doesn't spread his feet too far apart, which makes him less wristy and produces a wider backswing—Chi-Chi's is almost **U**-shaped. All the above are ways to avoid digging too deeply, the main

problem among average golfers in the sand.

Going to the ball, Chi-Chi pulls the club down with his left arm dominant. At the crucial moment just before and during impact, the clubhead has not passed his hands. Also, he keeps his knee flex throughout the swing, which is very important. Because of these moves, and because everything but the blade is aimed left, Chi-Chi can slip the clubhead neatly under the ball, taking a nice shallow divot. Thus his shots always come out with a lot of "stuff," stopping well and always spinning to the right—further indication of the good cutting action he imparts through impact.

Most bunker-play instruction,

incidentally, talks about cutting across the ball from outside to inside the target line, and usually says or implies that you must take the club back on the outside to do this. That's wrong, because it promotes a too-upright backswing and too deep a dig into the sand. Even if you get the ball out at all, it will have less bite and most likely will be misdirected.

When you take an open stance in the bunker, with the left foot drawn back well left of the target, the swing plane is *naturally* going to go across the target line from outside to in. You don't have to make an extra effort to do this, so just take the club back, as Chi-Chi does, along the normal path, or what feels like the normal path.

A STROKE OF VENTURI

In the Bunkers

Don't aim two or three inches behind the ball, as so much bunker instruction says, and then hit down into the sand. Do that and more often than not the ball will stay in the trap or, if it does get out, will lack height and spin.

An exercise: Put a tee in the sand beneath the ball just deep enough so that the ball does not sit on it. Now, in playing the shot, try to get the tee out of the sand. Practice that and you'll learn to make a nice cut through the sand.

A couple of other things about bunker play. First, the length of your follow-through determines how far the ball will go on an explosion shot. Second, you "blade" the ball, "skull" it, hit it "thin" or "clean" because you have not retained the flex in your knees throughout the swing.

A STROKE OF VENTURI

On Practicing

When you hit a good shot on the practice tee, don't immediately start another ball. Watch the shot to its very end, until it stops rolling, to give yourself the benefit of that time to retain the feel of the swing and to remember just what you did to achieve it.

I don't recommend trying to hit the same shot over and over again, because that way you tend to become a kind of robot and forget what you're doing. Try to do something different with one out of every five or six balls —hit high, low, a fade, a draw.

I think that if you're mentally alert, you can make your body perform properly no matter how tired you may be physically. So quit practicing only when you're mentally tired. And if you don't come away from the range feeling mentally exhausted, it hasn't been a good session.

A STROKE OF VENTURI

A Good Golf Shot Is a Vision

I have never hit a good shot that I didn't see first in my mind, in my imagination.

BEN CRENSHAW

Ben is the one man to analyze on the putting game, not only because he is so good at putting, but because his style reflects the kind of greens we generally play on nowadays. His way of putting also conforms to my primary principle for good golf, which, I'm sure you know by now, is proper posture. I believe the putting stroke is a miniature of the full golf swing.

1

2

The swing is not as long, of course, and the body doesn't turn, but in the impact zone the stroke is, or should be exactly the same in all other principals.

For most of golf history, right up to when I was a young player, putting greens were generally on the slow side, and not particularly smooth-rolling. This was especially true in the South, where a lot of the tour was played and where the greens were of native Bermuda grass. To putt them at all well, players of my generation and before developed one of two strokes. There was the short-backswing punch or pop stroke, of which Billy Casper's is a very good example, and there was a

3

4

longer, sweeping stroke from inside to out, a hooked putt that had a lot of overspin. Walter Hagen and Gene Sarazen putted this way, and with very heavy putters, but Bobby Lock had the most exaggerated strokes of this type I've ever seen—and how it worked for him!

Beginning in the late 1950s, however, there were some big advances in golf course agronomy and maintenance, and putting greens began to improve tremendously. Not only did they hold approach shots better, which has had much to do with the way today's young tour pros play approach shots—high and hard—but they also became smoother and faster for putting. And as this happened, so putters in the Ben Crenshaw mold developed.

The Crenshaw stroke is fairly long in both directions, the blade going back from and through the ball about the same distance either side and with no extra clubhead acceleration at impact. In other words, it is almost a perfect pendulum stroke. The blade is kept absolutely square throughout—no hooding over. Notice in pictures 3 and 4 that Ben's hands are in exactly the same position as they were at address. There is not even much wrist break on his backstroke.

This type of stroke is best accomplished by moving only the shoulders and arms, and the best way to achieve that is to have the arms hanging as straight and relaxed as possible. And the easiest way to do *that* is to stand more upright or "taller" at the ball, and not too close to it.

Crenshaw bends over just enough to comfortably reach the ball with his putter head. The players of my era, including myself, tended to bend more, to get our heads lower when putting. We did that because the short, punchy stroke needed then pretty much dictated it, and also because we were never quite certain what a putt would do: bounce, hit a snag, go left or right. When you're not sure of things you usually hunch up, get tight and cramped. Naturally, this created a crimping of the arms and, of course, some muscle tension you don't need for so delicate a business as putting. I must say that Ben Crenshaw's putting style requires smoothness and good nerves, but I think those qualities can be more readily developed when you're putting on today's smooth and consistent carpets.

I'm sure a lot of you do not putt all the time on the fast, smooth greens the pros usually enjoy on today's tour; many courses that get heavy play keep their greens a little long. But in general, we all putt on surfaces that have some speed and regularity, so I recommend the Crenshaw style.

The upright putting stance, by the way, is also advantageous in that you get to see the line better; there's less chance of your head getting out beyond the ball, which would cause you to lose perspective. It also keeps you from getting your weight on your toes, which can cause you to move your body during the stroke.

Remember that to putt like Crenshaw, the only things that should move are the arms and shoulders, with the hands very quiet.

A STROKE OF VENTURI

You *Do* Putt for Dough

Most golfers who get great pleasure out of shotmaking—hitting cuts, draws, high and low shots, etc.—don't like to putt. To them, it's boring. Ben Hogan was one such. He thought putting was another game, not really golf. He won so much because he hit so many shots close to the hole, which most people can't do.

I have to admit I never practiced my putting enough. I was always out hitting shots, *and was never more than an average putter on tour.*

But I've learned from that. When I teach kids to play golf now, I put them on the back tees. I don't want them to hit a lot of greens. I want them to be short so they have to learn early on how to pitch, chip, and putt. Whether that's golf or not, it sure has a lot to do with the game's bottom line.

A STROKE OF VENTURI

On Being "Up"

There's an even better reason for hitting a putt hard enough to get it to the hole, or past the hole, beside the obvious fact that it won't go in otherwise. If your putt goes by the hole you have gotten a complete read of the line, and the putt coming back is going to be easier for that.

A STROKE OF VENTURI

On Chipping

The best chippers are low-ball chippers. Except when the ball is sitting in long grass, or you have to get it up over a rise, you should use clubs with not much loft—the 5-, 6- and 7-irons—so there is minimal risk of the clubface slipping under the ball too much. Also, the more lofted the club, the harder it is to gauge how much the ball will run after it lands. With less lofted clubs the shot is more like a putt, and therefore easier to both gauge and execute.

A STROKE OF VENTURI

On "One-thought" Golf

Bobby Jones once said, when asked what he thought about while playing, "I think about the last things that worked."

Afterword

On the first day of our collaboration on this book, Ken Venturi and I were walking along the practice tee at Augusta National Golf Club, looking at the swings of players in the 1980 Masters tournament. Ken wanted to make his initial analyses of the pros "live." We would walk along more than a few other practice tees on the tour for the same purpose, and in each instance Ken was insightful and pointed in his comments. I knew he would be, for his reputation as a golf analyst preceded him, at least in my own case, many years before he became nationally celebrated for these skills through television.

Still, at Augusta National that day I was taken anew not only with Ken's quickness of mind, but his knack for noting the smallest details *vis-à-vis* the art of golf. One example: As we strolled along the practice tee, Ken stopped at the bag of Artie McNickle, the young California touring pro, who was not present at that moment. In the time-honored way of golfers, Ken pulled a club out of Artie's bag, set in on the ground, waggled it a few times. It happened to be an 8-iron. He put that back, took out a 9-iron and went through the same ritual. Then Ken said to me, "I haven't seen Artie play for a while and haven't talked to him lately, but I can tell you something about how he's hitting his short irons now. See if I'm right."

When McNickle appeared, after the greetings Ken said to him, "You've been hooking your short irons, got them turning over to the left. Probably pushing the other irons, in compensating."

Artie McNickle is an expressive fellow under most circumstances, but this time he just stared at Ken, his mouth slightly agape. He nodded his head and said, "That's dead right. How did you know?"

"The lie on your eight and nine irons is a little too upright. Maybe a degree. The toe is catching the ground first and turning the blade in," Ken explained.

McNickle blinked a few times and offered a small, incredulous smile. He took out his 8-iron, looked down at it, and shook his head. That evening he took it and the 9-iron to a club repairman in Augusta whom Ken recommended. The next day, after his round, Artie stopped Ken and told him he had just hit some of the best short irons of his life, and was hitting the other irons better too.

Little wonder Ken Venturi has become the most sought after "doctor" on the tour, the man the pros are going to for help, be it a quick once-over or an extended series of lessons.

In the course of gathering the material for this book, Ken dropped many more such insights on golf technique. Many of these gems came to his mind while describing the mechanics of Tom Watson's swing, or Jack Nicklaus's, Tom Purtzer's, Bill Kratzert's, and so on. Ken has that kind of mind, and style of thought: intuitive, quickly perceptive. It is his nature, but a nature seasoned by deep training. He recalled to me that in the years just before he joined the pro tour he practiced daily at the California Country Club, and after hitting five or six bags of balls would go into the locker room, lie on a bench, close his eyes and "put the feeling I had on the tee into my body."

And, of course, this Zenlike ingestion of golf sensitivity into every bone and sinew would pay off. As Ken went on to say, about his 1964 U.S. Open victory when he almost collapsed from heat prostration in the oven that was Washington, D.C., "I won by instinct. I looked at the shot and my body performed. Which is why I could do it even though I was completely exhausted."

Ken Venturi has had a remarkable career in golf—or in life for that matter. As a young boy he had a terrible speech defect, a stammer so embarrassing he became something of a loner. "I couldn't talk to anyone, so I just went out by myself and hit golf balls all day."

Perhaps it was the self-confidence he developed in becoming so brilliant a golfer that helped Ken overcome the stammer, and, ironically enough, to become a most articulate golf television commentator for CBS. It is a wonderful thing to turn a disability into an asset.

However, another physical problem would be visited upon Ken Venturi. After his dramatic U.S. Open victory in 1964 he lost the circulation in his hands and his serious playing career was soon terminated. He continues to play golf, of course, and quite well indeed, I can tell you. The swing he makes now is not quite the same as it had been. Because of his hands it is a bit shorter and flatter. But he has not forgotten how he did it in his prime, and it is that swing, which many knowledgeable golf people have said was one of the finest the game has ever had, which informs this book.

There is no better way to prove this than to present that Venturi swing in the following sequence, taken in 1962. To follow its pattern is to know that Ken Venturi is what he is always perceived to be, a man of his word.

—AL BARKOW
Upper Montclair, N.J.

KEN VENTURI